# THE KING'S HENCHMAN

BY THE SAME AUTHOR

THE HARP-WEAVER AND OTHER POEMS

RENASCENCE AND OTHER POEMS

A FEW FIGS FROM THISTLES

SECOND APRIL

❦

ARIA DA CAPO

TWO SLATTERNS AND A KING

THE LAMP AND THE BELL

THREE PLAYS

❦

# The King's Henchman

## A Play in Three Acts

### by Edna St. Vincent Millay

HARPER & BROTHERS PUBLISHERS
NEW YORK AND LONDON
MCMXXVII

To
**Eugen Jan Boissevain**

# THE KING'S HENCHMAN

## A Play in Three Acts

TIME: Tenth Century
PLACE: England

# PERSONS

EADGAR, King of England

DUNSTAN, Archbishop of Canterbury

ÆTHELWOLD, Earl of East Anglia, foster-brother and friend to Eadgar

ORDGAR, Thane of Devon

GUNNER
CYNRIC
BRAND
INGILD } Lords at the Hall of King Eadgar
WULFRED
OSLAC

MACCUS, servant and friend to Æthelwold

THORED, Master-of-the-Household to Ordgar

HWITA, Cup-bearer to the King

A BLACKSMITH

A SADDLER

A MILLER

A FISHERMAN

ANOTHER FISHERMAN

AN OLD MAN

ÆLFRIDA, Daughter to Ordgar

HILDEBURH
OSTHARU
GODGYFU } Ladies at the Hall of King Eadgar
LEOFSYDU
MERWYNNA

ASE, servant to Ælfrida

ENID, wife of Thored

A BLACKSMITH'S WIFE

A MILLER'S WIFE

A FISHERMAN'S WIFE

A NEAT-HERD'S WIFE

A WOMAN-SERVANT

ANOTHER WOMAN-SERVANT

A YOUNG GIRL

WYNNA, a child, daughter of Thored

Other lords and ladies, attendants, cup-bearers, villagers, fishermen, etc.

# THE KING'S HENCHMAN

## ACT I

[*Hall of* KING EADGAR *at* Winchester. *A great room
of gray stone, with small windows deep-set in the wall,
and massive doors. On one side of the room, at the
spectator's left, stands a long table of oak, roughly
carved, at the further end of which is a handsome,
high-backed wooden settle, and along the sides of which
run wooden benches without backs. In the middle of
the room a fire of logs is burning on a round open grate
of blackened stones; this fire has been burning for a
long time; the logs are thin in the middle, and glow
from end to end. There is no chimney; the smoke is left
to find its way out through cracks in the ceiling and
doors. Near the fire is a wooden settle. In the right
wall there is a door leading out to the stables. In the
center of the back wall is a broad double door leading
into the courtyard.*

3

*It is five o'clock of a morning about the end of
September. Through the thick glass of the small windows a pale daylight enters, but makes little headway
in the room, which is lighted now by tall rush torches,
and by a double row of candles running the length of
the table. The table is laden with a variety of meats
and loaves on heavy trenchers, together with cups and
goblets, mostly of horn, some few of thick glass.
Everything is in that disorder which attends the end
of a banquet: goblets overturned, dripping mead upon
the hard earth of the floor; a boar's head with little to
identify it but the two strong tusks; remnants of pig
and venison; bag puddings; wild-honey combs; and
rinds and scraps of white and yellow cheese.*

*At the head of the table, on the high-backed settle,
sits* KING EADGAR, *a dark man, short, stockily built,
with a handsome head, black hair, and a black beard.
He is less than twenty-five years old, but his thoughtful
face, grave eyes, and dignified bearing give him the
appearance of being somewhat older; he has been a
king for ten years, and shows it.*

*On the right of* EADGAR *is seated* DUNSTAN, *Archbishop of Canterbury, a man of forty, clean-shaven,
with a pale face and bright gray eyes, wearing his
house cassock, a black robe with purple at the neck.*

4

*During most of the act* DUNSTAN *talks to* EADGAR
*earnestly.*

*On* DUNSTAN'S *right sits* BRAND; *on* BRAND'S *right*
GUNNER, *a slim, worldly man, with a keen, gay face.*

*On* EADGAR'S *left is a vacant place. Next the
vacant place is* OSLAC, *a fat fellow, sound asleep,
with his head on the table.*

*At the foot of the table are two places; that on the
right is vacant; the other is occupied by* INGILD, *a big
man with blue eyes and a rick of red hair. The other
places are filled by* CYNRIC, WULFRED,—*a round-
faced boy of sixteen, who has already swung his ax
against the Danes in Yorkshire—and several other
lords, in various stages of intoxication,—one sleepy,
another sad, another argumentative.*

*Nearly all present are men between the ages of six-
teen and thirty; in these times only yokels lived to
grow old. They are dressed for the most part in skins,
with kilts and sleeveless jackets of rough woolen stuff,
and hose strapped from ankle to knee with deerskin
thongs.* EADGAR *is dressed much like the others,
except for a cloth cape heavily embroidered in rich
colors, which is fastened at his shoulder by an enamel
brooch, and a signet-ring of heavy gold.*

*On the right side of the room, not seated, but leaning*

against the doorway or half-sitting in the window recess, is a group of ladies, several of them wives of lords at the table. The matrons may be distinguished from the maidens by the fact that their hair, in the few instances when it is not hidden under a cap, is seen to be cut short; the unmarried women wear their hair down their backs, usually in two braids, and no cap, but only a narrow fillet about the forehead.

The ladies are not guests at the feast, but have been permitted to steal in to hear the songs of the harper. They keep themselves well in the background, not timorously, but as a matter of course, whispering among themselves. One or two have embroidery frames; when nothing else is going forward to arrest their attention, they bend their heads and stitch.

At the rise of the curtain MACCUS, trusty servant and true friend of Æthelwold, and also the most skillful and beloved harper for many shires about, is seated on a stool in the center of the stage, singing to the accompaniment of his harp. He is a man whose life has miraculously been preserved to the age of nearly fifty, scarred with battle wounds, with grizzled hair and beard and a rich, deep voice. He has been singing for over an hour the familiar and favorite saga of the glory and death of Cynewulf, King of Wessex long *ago, who, under cover of darkness, was treacherously put to death at the door of his mistress by a rival for the throne. All faces, save those of Oslac and one or two others, sunken in sleep, are turned earnestly toward* MACCUS. *The men lean forward across the table, their fists clenched, their jaws set; the women stand with their hands clutched to their breasts or hovering at their lips, in rapt and passionate attention.*]


MACCUS

[*Singing to the accompaniment of a harp*]

. . . Wild as the white waves
Rushing and roaring,   Heaving the wrack
High up the headland;   Hoarse as the howling
Winds of the winter,   When the lean wolves
Harry the hindmost,   Horseman and horse
Toppled and tumbled;   So at the town gate,
Stroke upon stroke,   Sledging and slaying,
Swashes the sword,   Shivers the shield
Of foeman and kinsman:   Such was the fight!
But lustless and lank   By the bower of the Lady,
Quenchèd forever,   Quellèd and cold,
Cynewulf the King!

7

LADIES

Woe-worth-the-day!

LORDS

[*Beating the table*]

Ho!  Ho!  Ho!
Maccus, man!  Maccus!  Maccus!

THE LADY OSTHARU

Oh, sorrow!  Oh, sorrow!

BRAND

Those were the days!
I tell you, take it deep and shoal,
Those were the days!

THE LADY HILDEBURH

Weep, weep for Cynewulf, wretched King!

CYNRIC

Mark ye, not a man of all his men
Was handy to help him!

GUNNER

Not they, the fat swine!  Rooting in the kitchen
    for mast!
Nuzzling i' the mash-vat!

THE LADY GODGYFU

Now hath his Lady a bitter burthen to thole!

8

LADIES

Yea, so!   Yea, so!

LORDS
[*Beating the table*]

Maccus, man!   Maccus!   Maccus!
Ho!

LORDS AND LADIES
[*Singing*]

Be the day far off,
O Harper!
When thy harp is unstrung!
Far off!   Far off!
Be that day,
O Singing Man!
Far off, O Harper!
When thy harp is unstrung!
And thy hand still!
And thy song sung!

KING EADGAR

Now, by the mead of Odin, a good tale, mightily
    told!
Come hither, Maccus, and slake thee!
Thou hast a throat like a corn kiln, or I'm a
    Welshman.

If but thy belly be as deep as thy lung,
Thou wilt not spit i' the cup.
Hwita! A stoup here!

Lord, and how sorrow-sweet, for all thy manly
    wounds,
Thou sangest the white Lenten-tide,
And lover from his leman sundered,—
Thou bearded nightingale!

### Maccus

It was the harp that sang, O Shield of Albion;
Not I.

[*He returns to his seat beside* Ingild, *at the foot of the
    table.* Hwita *fills a goblet for the King, then a
    cup for* Maccus. *Other cup-bearers go the
    rounds of the table.*]

### Cynric

Ho, Oslac!
Thou'lt fall into thy cup!

### Gunner

No fear, my friend:
The cup has long since fallen into Oslac.
        [*Laughter from the others*]

OSLAC

[*Waking up, drunkenly*]

Where's Æthelwold?

BRAND

Hast thou looked under the board for him?

GUNNER

*Under* the board?   He cannot see above it,
From where he sits!

[*Roars of laughter*]

WULFRED

Let 'em not feaze thee, Oslac, my lad; sleep on.

[*The lords continue to laugh and jest among themselves.
On the other side of the room the ladies are gossiping.*]

THE LADY HILDEBURH

[*To* GODGYFU]

Who is the woman, then?

GODGYFU

[*A dark, handsome girl, more than a little in love
with the King*]

Good shrift, *I* know not!

*11*

OSTHARU

[*Looking up from her embroidery*]

The woman is daughter to Ordgar, Thane of Devon.
"Ælfrida," she hight.

GODGYFU

I wonder the King sendeth not to Damascus for his
    bride!
Why stand at Devon?

HILDEBURH

'Tis said she is rankly fair.

GODGYFU

'Tis said of others.

OSTHARU

And I ween the chest of silver mancuses
Beside her father's bed
Doth not bedim her, neither.

HILDEBURH

Is he so rich in silver, the old man?

OSTHARU

Dear lady, he dare not stand too nigh the fire,
Lest he melt in his hose
And come out candlesticks!

[*They all titter for a moment at the picture thus pre-
sented, all except* GODGYFU.]

GODGYFU

[*Rising, and going to join another group of women*]
Howe'er it be,
And be she rich as silk,
Eadgar will naught of her,
If she be not fair as the moon.

[*At the table* EADGAR *and several of the lords are arguing with the Archbishop.*]

EADGAR

Sooth, Dunstan, a man will do much to keep his
        living,—
Much, but not all.

GUNNER

And the day thou swearest thy clergy into monks
Thou wouldst do well to widen thy doorstep:
For next year's crop of fatherless babes in England
Will be thicker than wolves in Wales!

INGILD

Yea, so.  "The sow will wallow in her filth
After she is washed"!

WULFRED

Heed him not, Dunstan.
Heed him not; or make a monk of him.

*13*

INGILD

Nay, Dunstan.   My gifts be otherwise.

GUNNER

Time will make monks of us all.

[*These last remarks have been greeted by roars of laughter.*]

DUNSTAN

Ah me,
In what a wilderness,
And snuffled at by wolves,
Build I the house of God!

WULFRED

Art wroth with us, father?

DUNSTAN
[*Quietly*]

No.
The Church of God is not a candle.
Blow on.

[*On the other side of the room the ladies are looking at a cloth which* OSTHARU *is embroidering.*]

LEOFSYDU

Lor', what a lovely fowl!
Look, Hildeburh!
Is it a pea-cock?

*14*

OSTHARU

Yea.

'Tis a wretched thing.

I cannot get the feathers o' the neck.

HILDEBURH

Mark the rich hue of his eye!—

Is it done with madder?

OSTHARU

I know not, Hildeburh.   I would I did.

'Tis some outlandish dye.

My brother brought it me from Flanders.

HILDEBURH

From Flanders, truly?   Belike from Ghent itself!

OSTHARU

Yea, so he said.   From Ghent in Flanders.

HILDEBURH

Think of it . . . think of it. . . .

By my heart, I would strip me bare of all I own,

And peddle pins for bread,

Might I but once take ship, and get a sight

Of Ghent in Flanders!

LEOFSYDU

Yea, 'tis a shining town.

'Tis a town to dream on.

*15*

MERWYNNA

[*Leaving another group and coming up to join them*]

Have ye heard the newest?

HILDEBURH *and* OSTHARU
[*Together*]

What's the newest, then?

MERWYNNA

Know ye the King doth send Lord Æthelwold
To fetch him home his bride?

HILDEBURH

Thou'rt not in earnest?

MERWYNNA

Yea, truly.

OSTHARU

A pretty mess he'll make of it!

HILDEBURH

Is then a woman's heart a Danish town,
To be took by dint of sword?

LEOFSYDU
[*Softly*]

'Tis a sweet lad.
'Tis a sweet, frozen lad.

*16*

OSLAC

[*Waking up, and looking aggrievedly at the vacant place beside him at the table, drunkenly*]

Where's Æthelwold?
I had my head on his shoulder.

GUNNER

Then 'tis the first head lay ever on his shoulder,
If tales be true.

CYNRIC

Nay, 'tis a known thing.
He maketh no bones of it.
Bold heart and a doughty arm in the fight he hath—
And in sooth his name alone in the Cambrian twi-
    light
Will gast the Harlech bairn—
Yet for all that, and all that,
At the Hall of King Love
Not yet is he dubbed Rider!

INGILD

Yea, so.    'Tis true as doom.
He shunneth a fair maid
As she were a foul-marten.
And should a wench but breathe upon him i' the
    dark,

17

He would bury himself till the smell of her were
    off him.

### GUNNER

'Tis a toothless babe the King sends into Devon
To bite his shilling.

### BRAND

Belike.  But 'tis a babe will fetch the shilling home
Sound in his fist, though fire and flood betide;
Nor lose it on the road; nor yield it up
To any forty reavers may beset him;
Nor spend his nights a-shining of it on his own
    sleeve.
And that is somewhat.

### CYNRIC

Yea, by my sword, 'tis much.
Sithen they were lads
Such trusting love doth live betwix these two
As singeth like a bird on a bough.
Light need or heavy need, the King in all things
Doth turn to Æthelwold, as he to Eadgar.
The heathen on his heath, into whose windy ear no
    whisper
Of Christian god-spell yet hath come,

*18*

Hath heard the tale of Eadgar and the wounded
     boar,
And Æthelwold's great love, to which the King
Doth owe his life.   How on the slope of Brecon
Eadgar, having sent his spear and found the grunt-
     ing wight
Full in the shoulder,—whereat the boar came at
     him,
Foaming and wroth—did nimbly step aside;
And how a hemlock put out its braided foot
And trapped him, and he fell, and the sickening
     breath
Was in his nostrils, and the tusk was at his throat;
So that he called out, "Brother!" and Æthelwold
Came running, and leapt upon them, throwing his
     wolf-skin
Over the little blood-shot eyes, and in his arms
Hugging the great head backward, said,
"Have out my knife and do him to the heart";
Which the King did.

[*There is a silence.*]

### BRAND

Fear for the King's life
He knoweth.   But as for himself,

He knoweth not Fear by sight; he hath not seen
Her shadow on a wall.

[*Enter through the door in the right* ÆTHELWOLD, *and
crosses to the fire. As he passes the ladies, they
look up, and follow him with gentle eyes. He is
a fair, beardless youth, slender, but muscular and
strong, seemingly younger than* EADGAR, *although
in fact his foster-brother.*]

CYNRIC
[*To* ÆTHELWOLD]

Ho, there thou art!
Talk of the Evil One, and thou treadest on his tail!
[EADGAR *looks up, and lifts his hand in affectionate
greeting to* ÆTHELWOLD, *who smiles, and lifts
his hand in reply.* EADGAR *returns to his conversation with* DUNSTAN.]

BRAND
[*To* ÆTHELWOLD]

Come back and be friendly!

CYNRIC

What's all this hopping up and rushing out and
tweaking of saddle-straps,—
As thou hadst never foot in stirrup ere this day!

20

GUNNER

Thinkest thou thy drink will stand forever steadfast
'Twix two such reavers as the Church and the King?

BRAND

[*Reaching across the table for* ÆTHELWOLD'S *cup,
and turning it bottom up*]

Nay, I'm the thief.
Sooth, Æthelwold, a man's a man,
E'en in these ladylike days,
And the little time a Saxon hath to himself,
What with kissing the Welsh and cuddling the Danes,
He owes to English drinking!

ÆTHELWOLD

[*At the fire, warming his hands*]

'Tis nigh daybreak.
Ye'd not believe, sitting here like a folkmoot of moles,
How bright the world is without.

GUNNER

And thou, thou wouldst not believe, out there in
the barnyard,
Snuffing up the wind like a fox,
How good the ale is within!

ÆTHELWOLD

A little wind is running like a tide

Over the grass.   It maketh a marsh of the dooryard.
And the sweet stench of the loam riseth sharp and
    chill.

OSLAC
[*Drunkenly, staring at him*]

Æthelwold!
Come back here and sit down!

[ÆTHELWOLD *comes over to the table, amid laughter,
    and stands beside* OSLAC, *with his knee on the
    bench.*]

CYNRIC

Yea, friend.   Here's Oslac, drunk as a Dane, hath
    yelped in his sleep
He had his head on thy shoulder.

GUNNER

Thy maidenhood is at moot.

ÆTHELWOLD
[*Good-naturedly*]

As for thee, thou pike,
Thy mouth is open.   Shut it.

GUNNER

Thou'rt a hard man.
Wouldst have me drink through my nose?

22

WULFRED

[*To Æthelwold*]

Maccus hath sung us the Death of Cynewulf
    fairly—
And thou wert not here!

ÆTHELWOLD

He'll sing it me on the road.   As he hath done
Full many a time before,—and fairly.
Maccus! that cribber of thine hath whittled his stall
    all night,
And stands knee-deep in shavings.   Were he my
    horse,
I'd trade him off for an oaten loaf,
And throw the loaf to a dog.

MACCUS

[*Rising*]

That horse, my lord, is a good horse.   Only he hath
    a hunger
Beyond the understanding of men.
[*He goes toward the door.*]
Thou'lt see the day erelong we'll trade our shirts
For an oaten loaf; yea, for a burnt one.

ÆTHELWOLD

Look well to the saddle-wallets.

*23*

### MACCUS
#### [*At the door*]

Nay, my lord.  There'll be no dearth on the road.
We've a fother of meal and cheese and apples,
And ale to drown in.
Nay, nay,—it is those fishy days in Devon
I have in mind.
'Tis said they live on herrings and kippers there,
With the liver of a holy-but o' Sundays.
Lean fare for a meat-loving man.

[*He goes out, right.*]

### ÆTHELWOLD
#### [*To the King's cup-bearer*]

Hwita!
Where is the boy?

### HWITA
#### [*Hurrying forward with a jug of mead and a drinking-cup*]

Here, my lord!

### ÆTHELWOLD

Good.   Give it four legs, Hwita,
And let it walk to me by itself.

[HWITA *brings him a cup and fills it.*]

24

EADGAR

[*Joining Æthelwold at the fire*]

How goes it with the mare?

ÆTHELWOLD

Never better.
And champing to be off.

EADGAR

And with thyself?

ÆTHELWOLD

Sooth, as for me—

[*He pauses, then bursts out in a troubled voice*]

I'd ride to hell for thee, and thou knowest it,
    Eadgar!
I'd be thy henchman to the Fiend himself!—
And call it but a half-day's run.
But as for Devon, I am not the man to send!

EADGAR

I know thou'rt loath to go.
Nor would I ask it of thee, Æthelwold,
But being so beset with irksome business
I cannot stir from my stool—and 'twix thee and
    me,

25

[*Glancing at the Archbishop*]

A scurf upon these clerks of Dunstan!
By Odin's foot, I am fed to the neck with them!—
Being, as I say, so teased with this and that,
I am stowed here for the winter in Winchester,
I have called upon thee, that are my milk brother
　　and my more than brother,
To ride out in my stead.

### ÆTHELWOLD

I am not unmindful, Eadgar.
And I would thou hadst need of my heart to throw
　　to thy hound:
Thou shouldst have it.
I speak no idle word.
But as for Devon,—I am not the man to send!
How shall I say a woman is foul or fair?—
So many dry leaves in a ditch they are to me,
These whispering girls,
A little fairish and a little foulish,
And all alike, and mightily underfoot!

### EADGAR

'Tis for that I send thee.
Thou art not like to go giddy and swoon from
　　horse

26

At the first wimple thou sightest on a Devonshire
    down.
Whom should I send in thy stead,—a man like
    Ingild?—
That recketh not if a wench be crippled or straight,
So she be warm-hearted?

Lo, thou,—I am sad, ywis, of my widowed lot,
And would be wed again.
But not to the first red kirtle thou'lt meet on a
    market-day,—
Else wherefore turn from home?

Sad of it.
Sad of it.
I would be wed again.
Nor have the world run clucking to its window,
"Come quick!  'Tis the King's leman!
The bold thing, look at her!
Stepping so proud, the brothel!"

Lord, I am lonesome for a lovely woman
To buy things for!
Bright silk that clashes like a sword!
And gems from the East, not seen before in England!

And weigh her down with them, that she might not
    walk
But leaning on mine arm.
Ah, Æthelwold,
What dost thou think on, in the Lenten-tide,
When the white thorn blossoms in the haw?

ÆTHELWOLD

I think on the Lenten-tide,
And the white thorn.
[*He is silent a moment.*]
Well, be it as thou wilt.
And by my winding-sheet,
I'll do my best for thee.
Yet, if I fetch thee home a gallèd filly
With dock-burrs in her mane,
Thou'lt thank me sparingly.

EADGAR

Thank thee, thou miller's thumb?—
I'll wed thee to the wench!

Come, knowest thou thine errand by heart?—
Say it over to me, then

ÆTHELWOLD

Know I mine errand?
28

Thinkest thou a man hath a nightmare pawing his
    chest
All night for nigh three sennights,
And knoweth not if she be iron-gray or dun?
So runs it:
I climb to my saddle and I ride and I ride and I ride,
Till I come to the gate of the house of the Thane
    of Devon.

### EADGAR

In sooth.

### ÆTHELWOLD

I knock at the gate, and I say to the Thane,
"Good day, good Thane.  Is thy daughter in?"
She's bound to be in;
Women never go out.

### EADGAR

In sooth.

### ÆTHELWOLD

I say to the daughter, "Good morrow, good maid.
Eadgar, son of Edmund, a loutish lad,
But a worthy chapman, hath heard thou art fair.
Now if thou be fair as men say thou be,
Then do on thy hood and hop to saddle with me;

29

And sooner than a weasel can suck a duck's egg
Thou wilt be Queen of England!"

EADGAR

In sooth.

[*He is silent, sunk in thought.*]

In sooth.

[*He rises slowly.*]

Æthelwold,—
Wilt thou pledge me?

ÆTHELWOLD

[*Leaping to his feet*]

Pledge thee, Eadgar!
Yea, so, by the Rood, will I!

EADGAR

Hwita!
Wine here!
In the cup of the Romsey nuns!

[*All the lords and ladies look up; and as* HWITA
*appears, handing to* EADGAR *a goblet of richly
fretted gold, they rise.* EADGAR *takes the cup,
holds it aloft, then offers it to* ÆTHELWOLD.]

30

ÆTHELWOLD

[*Lifting the cup to his lips*]

Wassail!

EADGAR

[*In the manner of the ancient ceremony, drawing his sword and holding it before* ÆTHELWOLD, *as if to protect him*]

Drink hale!

[*He strikes his sword into the ground between them.* ÆTHELWOLD *holds the cup aloft, then offers it to* EADGAR.]

EADGAR

[*Lifting the cup to his lips*]

Wassail!

ÆTHELWOLD

[*Drawing his sword and holding it before* EADGAR *as if to protect him*]

Drink hale!

[*He strikes his sword into the ground beside that of* EADGAR. EADGAR *gives back the cup to* HWITA. EADGAR *and* ÆTHELWOLD *clasp hands over the hilts of their swords.*]

*31*

LORDS *and* LADIES

[*With lifted arms, the men holding their drinking cups high*]

Wassail!

ÆTHELWOLD

[*To* EADGAR]

Now is thy Weird my Weird, and thy foe my fiend!

EADGAR

'Twix thee and wolfish want,
'Twix thee and sorrow,
'Twix thee and the singing arrow with the darkened
    fang,
I stand with open breast!

Life, that is stronger than I, is not so strong
As thou and I!

ÆTHELWOLD

Death, that is stronger than I, is not so strong
As thou and I!

TOGETHER

Unquellèd, thou and I,
Till Life and Death be friends!

32

LORDS *and* LADIES

Wassail!

[EADGAR *and* ÆTHELWOLD *sheathe their swords.*]

EADGAR
[*To* ÆTHELWOLD]

Come now and see the day,
If the sun be up!

[*They turn and walk toward the back of the stage.
Two doorkeepers run up and swing open the
heavy doors, revealing, immediately without, a
stoutly walled courtyard with a closed gate, and
beyond, an autumn countryside. It is bright
dawn.*]

ÆTHELWOLD

The eastern wall is astir and the gate ajar!

EADGAR

The night is done, my lords.
Blow ye the candles out!

ÆTHELWOLD
[*To* EADGAR]

Whiles thou and I blow out the morning star!

EADGAR

Up, Sun!   Stir in thy straw!

*33*

Night yawns, and sighs to give over the watch to
    thee!

ÆTHELWOLD

All saddled, all bridled, without thy gate,
Thy stallion, the milk-white wind—for the time
    grows late—
With silver hoof beginneth to stamp and paw!

EADGAR

We have saddled and bridled the wind for thee!
We have cut thee a whip from the withy tree!

ÆTHELWOLD

Up! Up! If thou'rt riding west with me!

EADGAR

Up, Sun! Stir in thy straw!

ÆTHELWOLD

Day breaks. I go.

[*To* DUNSTAN]

Thy blessing, father, upon me and upon mine er-
    rand.

DUNSTAN

[*Lifting his hands above* ÆTHELWOLD'S *head*]

Thee, my son,
I freely bless,

And commit unto the care of the Most High.
As for thine errand—

[*He drops his hands and turns away.*]

I would to my heart that wise and holy *magister*,
Paulus of Tarsus, in my humble stead might speak
Unto the King, that seeketh now a second wife!

[*With pain and passion*]

*Solutus es ab uxore?—ne quaere uxorem!*

### EADGAR
[*Lightly but earnestly*]

Yea, Dunstan, and I would thy Paulus of Tarsus
    were here to answer thee:
'*Tis better to wed than to burn!*

### DUNSTAN
[*In a low voice, turning away*]

I shout into the wind, that beareth my words
    nowhither, but only back
To mine own ear.

[*The men of* ÆTHELWOLD'S *retinue begin to ride past
    the door, singing, and draw up before the gate
    in the outer wall. During the song* EADGAR *and*
    ÆTHELWOLD, *with their arms about each other's
    shoulders, keep time by stamping the floor;*

Gunner *and the other lords, by beating with their drinking-cups upon the table.*]

MACCUS and Retinue

Oh, Cæsar, great wert thou!
 And Julius was thy name!
That furrowed thy way through a fallow spray,
 And to stormy Britain came!
But I would not stand in thy stead,
For I'd liefer be quick than dead!

ALL Men

But I would not stand in thy stead,
For I'd liefer be quick than dead!

EADGAR

Oh, Cæsar, great wert thou!

ÆTHELWOLD

 And Claudius was thy name!

EADGAR and ÆTHELWOLD [together]

That said, "To be rid of what Julius did,
 I'll go and do the same!"
But I would not stand in thy stead,
For I'd liefer be quick than dead!

ALL Men

But I would not stand in thy stead,
For I'd liefer be quick than dead!

ÆTHELWOLD

Oh, Cæsar, great wert thou!

EADGAR

And Hadrian was thy name!

ALL *Men*

Thine eye did itch till a Roman ditch
  Was dug in British shame!
But I would not stand in thy stead,
For I'd liefer be quick than dead!

ALL *Men and Women*

Cæsar, thy day is done!
Whiles ours is but begun!

[ÆTHELWOLD'S *mare is at the door, held by an attendant.   He goes up to her and throws his arm over the saddle.*]

ÆTHELWOLD

Farewell, all here!

[*The doorkeepers open the outer gate.*]

ALL

Farewell!
Fare thou well, and God be with thee!
Fair weather and good roads!
God keep thee from all fear!

God be with thee!
Farewell!

[ÆTHELWOLD *and* EADGAR *clasp hands.*]

ÆTHELWOLD

Ere the summer goose flies,
Thou shalt have word from Devon.

EADGAR

God keep thee, Æthelwold!

ÆTHELWOLD

God shield thee, my King!

[*He leaps to the saddle.*]

[*To all*]
Farewell!

ALL

Farewell!

[ÆTHELWOLD *turns his horse and rides briskly off
through the gate, followed by* MACCUS *and the
men of his train.*]

CURTAIN

# THE KING'S HENCHMAN

## ACT II

[*A forest in Devonshire.  A month later.  Through a dense fog the great shapes of oaks and beeches are dimly visible, with here and there the slender trunk of a birch, or the rounded clump of a holly tree.  It is the evening of All Hallow Mass.  The night is not dark, but faintly luminous, owing to the presence of a full moon striving to penetrate the fog.  Enter from the side, slowly, and looking about him like a man who has lost his way,* ÆTHELWOLD, *and stands, visible to the audience through a thin veil of mist.*]

ÆTHELWOLD
[*Calling*]

Maccus!

MACCUS
[*Invisible, but close at hand*]

My lord!

AETHELWOLD

Thou'rt nearer than I thought.
Findest thou aught of a road?

MACCUS

I find no road a weasel would follow to market,—
But as a short cut.
And thou?

AETHELWOLD

There was a road; but here sharply it diveth
Into the earth.
I know not where we are.   We are as lost
As we shall ever be.
Come hither, wilt thou?
[*He seats himself upon a fallen tree.*]
Here ran the road.
[*Musing*]
And here at my feet it diveth
Into the earth.
Can it be the woman is daughter to the Fiend,
And I must woo her in hell?

MACCUS
[*Somewhat further away*]

Ywis, my lord.
All women are daughters to the Dark One.

*40*

Spare only two.   And they—
[*He stumbles, and crashes into the bushes*]
And they [*somewhat further away*] be sisters to him.

ÆTHELWOLD

Maccus, thou'rt going from me!
Turn back!

MACCUS

From thee!
That's playful!
Am I a rush-light, that thou bobbest about me in
    the mist like a moth?

ÆTHELWOLD

Nay, friend, thou'rt turned about.
Come this way.

MACCUS
[*Nearer*]

Where art thou?

ÆTHELWOLD

Here!

MACCUS

Speak again.

ÆTHELWOLD

Here!

[*Pause.*]
There'd be a moon tonight,
Were it not for the mist.

MACCUS
[*Near by*]

In sooth.
There'd be a sun tonight,
Were it not otherwise.
My belly is windy with It-would-be-if-it-were-not!
Where art thou, i' God's name?

ÆTHELWOLD

Here!
[*The shape of* MACCUS *emerges from the fog.*]

ÆTHELWOLD *and* MACCUS [*together*]

I see thee!

ÆTHELWOLD
[*Stretching out his hands to* MACCUS]

Well met!
The mist is in thy beard.

MACCUS

As for thy beard,
I think 'tis in the mist, for I see it not!
[*He laughs.*]
Is this thy road to the Pit?

42

ÆTHELWOLD

Yea, Maccus.
What sayst thou to this?

MACCUS

I say that if this be the gateway to her bower,
Then is thy lady daughter to a fox!

ÆTHELWOLD

*My* lady, Maccus!—Bestow her not on me!

MACCUS

[*Gloomily*]

Yea, so.   Thy lady.

[*He seats himself on the log beside* ÆTHELWOLD.]

Thy lady to woo,
And the King's to wed.
So runneth the tale,
And 'tis a tale for madmen.
God wot, and I wot well, it is a tale for madmen.

ÆTHELWOLD

Lord, what a merry churl art thou
To be lost in a wood with!
What ails thee, man?

MACCUS

[*After a silence*]

My heart hath a stone in its shoe.

[*Pause.*]

ÆTHELWOLD

Friend, an thou hast a crumb of bread in thy scrip,
I'll play the sparrow to it.

MACCUS

[*Rising and unbuckling the wallet from his belt*]

I have, my lord; and a crumb of cheese as well;
Set by against this ebb.

ÆTHELWOLD

I could do mousily by a crumb of cheese.
Hast thou enough for two?

MACCUS

Yea, for two mice I have,
Or for two sparrows.

[*He lays out bread and cheese and ale between them.*]

ÆTHELWOLD

Why, 'tis a supper for a king!

MACCUS

It is, my lord.   A king in irons.

44

[*They eat.*]

Would we had left a clue of thread behind us.
Then might my goodwife wind me home to break-
    fast.
'Tis mealtime.

ÆTHELWOLD
[*Yawning*]

'Tis bedtime.

MACCUS
[*Presently*]

I'll have another look about for the men.
That is to say, a grope and a smell about.
That is to say, a blind man's look about.

ÆTHELWOLD

Go not far, I beseech thee, Maccus.  Bear in mind
The wood's bewitched with mist.

MACCUS

Fear not.  I'll fell an oak at every step,
To mark me back.

[*He goes out on the right.*]

ÆTHELWOLD

As for me, there's but one thing in the world I
    crave:

*45*

And that's to stretch me out along the moss,
And sleep from now to Lammas.

[*Going back up stage toward the right.*]

O darling Sleep, hast thou a word for mine ear?—
I will not shout thee down.

[*Invisible to audience.*]

Dog-tired I am.
Ah, this is good.
Say what ye will, the wild deer have the best of it.
There's an uncouth man for you, that Maccus,
That standeth up when he might lie down.
I'll be asleep ere mine arm be under my head.

[*Silence falls again upon the forest. The trees stand
   motionless in the fog. A few pale beech leaves
   circle slowly down. From somewhere on the left
   a sound is heard—the snapping of a twig. It
   is heard again, a little nearer—the small
   crash of a branch underfoot. Presently on the
   left a faint glow appears, as of a lamp in the fog.
   Then comes the sound of voices.*]

ÆLFRIDA
[*Off-stage*]

I'll go no further!
Had I known I was to wade,

I would have come barefoot.

Sawst thou ever the moss so sea-weed sodden wet?

ASE

[*Off-stage*]

Nay, sooth, my lady.

In all my born days never,

Not I.

I cannot say am I afloat or ashore.

[*Enter from the back on the left, slowly appearing through the fog, ÆLFRIDA, a mature girl of seventeen, lithe and tall. Her long hair, which is very fair in color, but not so much yellow as pale red, falls in bright waves over her shoulders, confined only by a silver fillet about the forehead. Her eyes are wide and dark, her scarlet mouth soft but imperiously set, her skin dazzling in its whiteness; she is beautiful. She is dressed in a soft, pale garment without sleeves, and wrapped in a dark cloak. Her movements are graceful and free, like those of an animal accustomed to find sure footing over difficult ground. Following ÆLFRIDA comes ASE, carrying a torch. ASE is a small dark woman of forty, with a sharp face.*]

47

ASE

They say, my lady, when 'tis thick on Hallow Mass
    Eve,
'Tis the steam from the witches' kettle.

ÆLFRIDA

The steam!—'tis the broth itself.

[*She looks about her.*]

Well, thou must go now, Ase.
Nay, bide a bit:
That spell of thine—will it work as well with the
    light?

ASE

Yea, better, if thou keep the light behind thee;
Then mayst thou see his shadow beside thine own
    on the mist;
As now, see thine and mine.

[*She holds the torch behind them.*]

ÆLFRIDA

[*Seeing the two shadows on the mist*]

Shield me! I should fall in a swoon!
Behind my back, thou sayst,—
That's knavish!

Yet better a knave of mine own
Than a knight of my father's choosing.
Well—thou must leave me, I think.

[ASE *turns to go.*]

Ase!—Art thou going?

### ASE

[*Pausing*]

Be not eery, my lady.
There's naught to harm thee here, in the shadow of
    thy home.
Many and many a maid
This Hallow Mass Day at Night,
Doth seek in spell and rune, even as thou,
Her lover that is to be.

### ÆLFRIDA

Yea, but not all
In such a mizzling mist!
I am not eery.
But I think I have been bolder—
In the daytime—
Indoors.
Go now, and go lively, Ase, for my marrow oozeth!

ASE

I leave thee the light.
[*She gives the torch to* ÆLFRIDA *and goes out on the left. Pause.*]

ÆLFRIDA

What am I doing here
In the dripping dark,
On the eve of All Hallows?
Ghosts alone
Of men long dead
And weanèd to the dripping dark
Will be abroad tonight;
And tittering elfin things,
To stroke me with their nails!
No lissome, laughing ghost
Of warm and living youth
Will rise from the ground at my spell!

How runneth the rune she taught me—
"White-thorn and black-thorn"—
Nay, I've lost it.   'Tis clean shunted off.

I wonder, had I done better to sit at home
And bide by the tidy fire
A tidy fireside love!

Or take, and be done with it, the thick and bum-
      bling churl
That my father hath in mind?

No, by my shift!
How runneth the rune?—
"White-thorn and black-thorn"—
I must stand with the light at my back—
[*She holds the torch behind her.*]
And God knoweth what beside I turn my back to!
"White-thorn—white-thorn—"
'Tis on the tip of my tongue—
[*She hesitates.*]
But my tongue is at the roof of my mouth!
I would I were yawning at home with my hands in
      my lap!

Bide a bit—so it goes!—
(I trust there's naught un-Christian in it;
I had meant to ask her.
Either way, I'm guiltless.
For I am unaware.)

[*She sings.   Whenever in the course of her song she
      comes to the word "holy-bough," she crosses her-
      self.*]

51

White-thorn and black-thorn,
Red haws in the hedge,
Sloes in the hedge, woad-black,
And a dusty dew on them;
Hairy stem
Of fennel,
Holy-bough and dill,
Dark yew;
Wormwood, woody nightshade,
And thy baleful sister, too!
 Show me in dream, yet nothing dim,
 The shadow and the shape of him!
 *All Hallows Eve is All Saints Morning!*

Thousand-blossom, white and red,
Spikèd willow-grass, wading-arrow;
I will lay him on my bed,
And bind his wounds with yarrow;
White-thorn, black-thorn, holy-bough, speed-well,—
Bind his wounds with yarrow.
 *All Hallows Eve is All Saints Morning!*

Seeds of poppy, small and black,
Borne to mill upon my back,
Into little loaves I'll knead,

For to bake him sleepy-bread;
Lest he leave me, lest he rise and leave me.
White-thorn, black-thorn, holy-bough, poppy-seed,
Bake him sleepy-bread.
*All Hallows Eve is All Saints Morning!*

Nettle, sheathe thy naughty smart,
Be of bristles callow;
Bind his heart upon my heart,
Withy of the sallow.
White-thorn, black-thorn, periwinkle, holy-bough,
Withy of the sallow!
*All Hallows Eve is All Saints Morning!*

White-thorn and black-thorn,
Thorn-apple, rank and reeking;
He shall drink mandragora,
Rooted up a-shrieking!
Holy-bough, white-thorn, holy-bough, black-thorn,
Holy-bough,
Mandragora!
*All Hallows Eve is All Saints Morning!*

Rise now in dream, yet nothing dim,
The shadow and the shape of him.

53

[*She holds the torch behind her at arm's length.   During the preceding song the fog has gradually been lifting, revealing a deep forest.   High in the distance is seen the lighted window of a house. Scarves of mist still cling about the bushes and trees, drawing out into ribbons and drifting slowly away. Here and there a tall trunk stands stark and clear, but the wood is in shadow, for the moon is under a cloud.   As* ÆLFRIDA *finishes her song, the cloud passes and a shaft of bright moonlight falls full upon* ÆTHELWOLD, *asleep at some distance from her, on a bed of emerald moss.*]

ÆLFRIDA

Ah!

What lieth yonder?

[*She lifts her hand to her lips and, staring at him, crushes out the torch in the wet leaves.   Then, leaning forward, she looks at him intently.*]

'Tis the play of the moon on the moss.


Nay.

It twisteth not awry,

Nor melteth into fallen bough and moss and moonlight.

*54*

[*She looks at him for a long time, then with a sigh lays her hand upon her heart.*]

Whatever thou art,
I would thou wert the thing thou seemest,
So lord-like,
So lank and young!

Mazèd in drowzy sleep he lies,
The small and childish locks about his brow
Bright in the moon, and crimpèd by the wet wind.

Beware! Beware!
No moonlight, but the wanton craft of witches
Hath wrought him!

Ah, that black evil hath might to build so fair!

My heart hath seen him, too.

Oh, heart, be wise!
Else mayst thou love forever in hunger and tears
A golden husk!

I must go quickly away from here.
I know, I know I am lost if I bide.
My head is wild with dreams.

Oh, darling thing unblest,
How shall I leave thy side?

*55*

Now is his hand in shadow.
Moon, how thou stridest,
And whippest up the clouds to foam about thy knees!
Ah, could I make him some way mine,
Ere night like a raven go flapping to another wood!
Some way, some way mine!

[*She steals closer and bends above him.*]

Oh, lief and lovely ghost,
When thou shalt wake, forget not—
As of a dream, yet ruddier than thy day—
Once in a mossy grove and moon-besprent
A breathing maiden
Did dearly, dearly love thee!
Oh, take with thee away,
To warm a little thy damp and chilly house,
This kiss I give thee,
For 'tis thine, 'tis thine!—
And heaven shrive my soul.

[*She kisses him swiftly, and rises to her feet.*]

ÆTHELWOLD

[*In his sleep*]

Oh no!
Oh no!

56

ÆLFRIDA

*[Moving fearfully away]*

Shield me, all Saints and Martyrs!

ÆTHELWOLD

*[Starting up, with his hand on his sword]*

Who's there?

*[ÆLFRIDA stands in the shadow of the trees, motion-
less. He goes up and peers into the shadow.]*

I see thee where thou hidest, and my sword hath
  got the wind of thee!

Slinking shadow, come forth into the light!—

Else mayst thou sing "Truce! Truce!" to the
  harrier-hawk

That whetteth his bill on thy thigh-bone!

ÆLFRIDA

I' the name o' God,

Forbear!

*[She comes out into the light. Her dark cloak falls
  from her shoulders. In her pale robe, silvered
  by the moon, she stands watching him guardedly,
  poised for flight.]*

ÆTHELWOLD

*[Slowly]*

What art thou?

What art thou, that hither from thy hollow hill
    art come
To work me woe?

Ah, and what spell is this upon me,
That I see thee through a glistering web
More softly bright
Than the silver stole of the moon?

Oh, thing unearthly fair,
What hast thou wrought upon me whiles I slept?
Whiles I slept. . . .
Ah, could I sink again into a dream I had. . . .
I think I knew thee better there.
Yea, so.
I knew thee there.

### ÆLFRIDA
[*In a low voice, turning and facing him*]
Thou knewest me never, never in this world,
Nor I thee.
All this hath the moon done.
And the moon will set.

Tomorrow's sun will find me what I am,
An earthly maiden, watching the cold sea
Go out and come in.
    *58*

Tomorrow's sun will find thee riding a far road,
An earthly man, light-hearted and free.
The sound of thy horse's hooves and the creaking
    of the saddle-leather
Will mind thee of many things,
But never of me.
Farewell.
We shall not meet again
In any wood,
In any weather.

ÆTHELWOLD

Oh, Godes Son!
How wounding fair thou art!
The sight of thee
Is like a knife at the heart.
Of thee the sight or the sound,
The turn of thy head, thy speaking,
Is like a thing found,
To a man seeking.

ÆLFRIDA

Too bright, too bright are thine eyes!
Stare not so upon me with thy wide-open eyes!

[*She covers her face with her hands.*]

59

ÆTHELWOLD

Now will I learn by heart thy hands
And the wanton way of thy hair, where thou bind-
  est it under.

[*She takes down her hands in confusion.*]

Nay, be not wroth with me;
Nor chide mine eyes.
Two children are mine eyes before thy shining
  wonder.

ÆLFRIDA

[*Catching up her cloak from the ground*]

I must be gone from here.
Farewell.
Forget thou sawst me ever.

ÆTHELWOLD

Nay—nay—and canst thou with thy summer-mouth
Utter these dry leaves?
Thou fillest the still house of my mind
With a shrill din,—
Tramping and singing, and the clashing of spear
  on spear!
The doors of my mind burst open from within,
And out throng the wild words!

*60*

Forget thee—
Men do not live so long!

ÆLFRIDA
[*Faintly*]

Be still . . . be still . . .
Oh, is it sleep or death whose drowsy mouth
Draineth my heart of blood? . . .
[*She looks into his eyes.*]
Let me go . . . let me go. . . .

ÆTHELWOLD

No, no—no, no—
Ah, thy sweet look,
Thine arrowy, sweet, sweet look!
'Tis sunk to the feather in my heart. . . .
Pluck it forth!   Pluck it forth! . . .
Oh, God, what aileth me?
[*He turns and leans his forehead against the trunk of
the tree by which he is standing.   Presently he
turns and looks at her.*]
Thou—knowest thou aught of love, and how it
taketh a man?
Thinkest thou I am in love with thee?

ÆLFRIDA
[*Faintly*]

I would it were so. . . .

*61*

ÆTHELWOLD

[*Staring at her*]

I must be near thee or die.

[*He comes blindly toward her and takes her in his
arms.*]

ÆLFRIDA

I am lost. . . . I am swept out to sea. . . .

[*She lifts her face to his.  He kisses her.  They stand
for a moment embraced.*]

How thou shakest!

Art thou a-cold, my dear?

ÆTHELWOLD

Yea . . . nay . . . I know not . . .

I am a tree in a storm. . . .

[*He turns from her, clinging to her hand, and sinks
down upon the fallen tree.*]

How silken-soft thou art,—

Wonderful . . . wonderful. . . .

How camest thou thus unwounded through the
brambly wood?—

The brambly world?

Look at me: I am woven all of sedges,

Like a rush mat.

62

ÆLFRIDA

Not so.

[*She spreads her cloak hastily over the log and seats
herself upon it beside him. She touches his cheek.*]

Thy cheek is brown and smooth,
Like the rind of a nut
New bursten from his burr.
I have not seen thy like.

ÆTHELWOLD

The like of thee
Sings not nor blossoms.

The wind that soughs in the sedges at the edge of
the pool
Has seen the swan go by,
So still and slow
And cool.

The bee that ferries his hoard from blossom to hive
Ere summer day be done,
Knows the sweet reek of the clover
Bruised by the wheels of the sun.

Wan ghost between
Two lights, the shadowy flutter-mouse,

Half-seeing and half-seen,
Swoops in the glimmering even;
The early star he knows,
And her cool wave upon his ribby fin.

Sweet, sweet,
Without, within,
Is the rose,
Whither the white moth steereth his sail.

Yet, ah, not wind nor bee
Nor any earthly wight
Hath seen what I see,
Nor hath any man heard from his father's father in
    an old tale
The like of thee.

ÆLFRIDA

Ah, me, how frosty sweet the moonlight!

ÆTHELWOLD

Icy sweet on thy mouth of ripened haws the moonlight. . . .
Belovèd . . . belovèd. . . .

ÆLFRIDA

Oh, darling head, shut out the moonlight from my
    mouth,
And kiss me in thy shadow!

64

ÆTHELWOLD

Drink, drink in haste my breath,
Ere it be swallowed up by thievish Death!

[*He kisses her. Presently her head falls back against
his shoulder.*]

ÆLFRIDA
[*Drowsily*]

O moon, draw not aside thy hem from this green
    moss
Ever, ever.

O droning Weird, let now thy busy spindle be at
    rest,
And do thou sleep awhile,
Thy shaggy head fallen forward upon thy breast.

O deep wood, unstill with small sounds,
Be kinsman to our love.
Nor let the chilly frost with his hoar rime
Creep up, creep up upon the drowsy summer
For yet a little time.

And ye, oak and beech,
With your dark boughs outspread,
Drop not your leaves, however shrunk and sere,
Upon a lover's hand, a lover's head.

*65*

Ere we find speech
For all this ache and wonder,
Oh, gast us not with the death of the year!

[*Suddenly she puts her arms about* ÆTHELWOLD'S
*neck and shrinks against him.*]

Ah, love, I fear a little, I fear, I fear
This fire we so recklessly kindled alone in the
woods at night!
Hungry, hungry about us on every hand
It leaps and spreads among the trees!
Far off in the deep wood the grazing stag,
With listening hoof and antlers high,
Stands now with blinded eyes ablaze,
Bewildered in its light!

I love thee so!  I love thee so!

[*She takes his face in her hands and kisses him.  Then
sleepily, once more, her head falls back against
his shoulder.*]

ÆTHELWOLD

Ah, could we hide us here in a cleft of the night,
And never be found!

ÆLFRIDA

Lost, lost,

Forgotten and lost,
Out of sight, out of sound!

### ÆTHELWOLD

Letting the sun ride by, with his golden helmet,
And all his flashing spears and his flags out-
      streaming,—
Ride by, ride by, ride by,
Shaking the ground!

### ÆLFRIDA

And never be found!

### ÆTHELWOLD

Letting the world ride by, jingling his pennies
And telling his beads;
Time, drawn by the snail and the hare,
Asleep in his rattling wain;
Sorrow, giving her horse his head,
Riding in the rain;
Death, bloody-spurred,
Astride his iron bird!—

### ÆLFRIDA

Ride by, ride by, ride by,
And never be found!

67

ÆTHELWOLD

Lost . . . lost. . . .

ÆLFRIDA

Forgotten and lost. . . .

ÆTHELWOLD

Out of sight. . . .

ÆLFRIDA

Out of sound. . . .

[*Her head is on his shoulder. Her eyes are closed.
They remain so for a moment, silent.*]


ASE
[*Off-stage, calling*]

My lady!

ÆLFRIDA
[*Startled, looks up. Pause*]

'Tis Ase.
'Tis my woman. I'd clean forgot her.
Yea, and my father . . . and my father's house. . . .
And all my life. . . .
I'd clean forgot.
I must be gone.
I do not know thy name.

ÆTHELWOLD

Nor I thy name.
"Æthelwold," I hight.

ÆLFRIDA

"Æthelwold."
'Tis the first time I speak thy **name**.
But not the last time.

ÆTHELWOLD

Nay.
And thou?

ASE
[*Off-stage, calling*]

Ælfrida!

[*At the sound of this name* ÆTHELWOLD *starts.*]

ÆLFRIDA

I must be gone!
"Ælfrida," I hight.
Is it uncouth to thee—"Ælfrida"?

ÆTHELWOLD
[*Shaken*]

No.   I have heard the name.

ÆLFRIDA

I must be gone.

*69*

I will come back in a little while.
[*She turns to go.*]

ÆTHELWOLD
[*With dread*]

Ælfrida!

ÆLFRIDA
[*Turning back*]

'Tis the first time thou sayst my name.
But not the last time.

ÆTHELWOLD

No.

ÆLFRIDA

What will my lord?

ÆTHELWOLD

Thy father—?

ÆLFRIDA

My father?   What of him?

ÆTHELWOLD

How hight he?

ASE
[*Off-stage*]

My lady!   My lady!

ÆLFRIDA

Good lack!   She'll be running hither!
"Ordgar," my father hight.
He is the Thane of Devon.
God be wi' thee.
Bide here, and I will come again.
[*She runs out, left.*]

ÆTHELWOLD
[*After a pause*]

I have not heard aright.
Never, since first the moon shone down upon the
    head of man,
Hath such an evil been wrought.
"Ordgar, my father hight.   He is the Thane of
    Devon."
Oh no!  Oh no!
I hear my tongue.
It shouteth, "No!"
But my heart saith not a word;
It only weeps.

And was it thou, then all this time?—
A name on the tongue, there in the hall of Eadgar,
A drifting shape in the mind, a dim, proud woman
In a golden snood . . . and it was thou.

71

Thou, all the long way hither. . . .
I ate and slept . . . and it was thou.
I woke and rode on again . . . and it was thou.

Ah, Life, I hate thee for thy stingy ways!
Thou art a chapman and a chafferer;
And cheapenest with thy meeching whine
Thy loveliest wares!
Thy bony brother Death
Hath to his name but a puff of dust in a potshard;
But what he has, he gives.

Ywis, a grim and iron God,
No friend of man, but a stalker and trapper of man,
Hath set this lime,
Wherein with besmearèd feet and feathers
I flutter and beat.

"Ordgar, my father hight. He is the Thane of
　　Devon."

Oh, dreadful dream, burst, burst! and let me out
　　of thee!

There is no way out.
Cursèd be this day!
And naked of grass and blossoms from this night
　　forth

The wreath of ground whereon in a breath of time
I found and lost my love!

[*He sinks down upon the fallen tree and drops his head
in his hands.*]

Now from my tears let the gray Weird water her
  ash tree.
Here sharply endeth and is seen no more
The golden thread in the woof.
From this day out, my life is a dingy web,
A threadbare thing,
A kirtle for a neat-herd.

So then, the tale of Æthelwold his love
Is nimbly told.

[*Enter* MACCUS *from the right.*]

MACCUS

My lord, the horses are at hand, full of grass;
And hard by is a road well trodden, that like as not
Hath been there all night.

ÆTHELWOLD

Speakest thou to me, friend?
Look again:
Thou sawst me never.

MACCUS

I saw thee never so down-i'-the-mouth and bleachèd,
If that be thy drift.
Thou'rt peaked as a garfish.
In God's name, what hath worn thee down?

ÆTHELWOLD

The teeth of Sorrow.   I am Sorrow's bone.

Done for.   Wantonly, scurvily done for.
Death is twins; and stareth upon me from two
    sides.
Maccus, thou seest me driven by a foe against whose
    fell
My sword is tallow.
Come, let me lean upon thine arm.
I am an old man;
For I am gutted of hope.

MACCUS

My lord, my lord, what hath come over thee?

ÆTHELWOLD

I have seen her.
I have seen my lady.
My lady—and the King's.

74

MACCUS

God above!   Oh, wretched boy!


ÆTHELWOLD

Take me away from here and set me on my horse.


MACCUS

Whither wendest thou?


ÆTHELWOLD

To Winchester.

Love, Love, how shall I wean me to thine ember-
days?

To Winchester.

Ere she be coming back and calling me,

My throstle-throat!   My lovely thing!

To Winchester . . . to Eadgar . . . to the King!


[*He runs out on the right, followed by* MACCUS.   *The
wood is quiet for a moment.*]


ÆLFRIDA
[*Off-stage, calling*]

Æthelwold!

75

Ase, thou oaf, [*gayly*]
Canst thou not wield thy legs?

ASE
[*Off-stage*]

I am numb with cold.
Frost-bit I am, from falling asleep i' the wooze.

ÆLFRIDA

Here, give me thy hand.
Lord! how thou creakest!
[*She laughs.*]
Never mind,—tear it loose!

Oh, Ase, when thou seest him, when thou seest him,
    girl. . . .
Words cannot build him,
How fair he is. . . .
[*Calling*]
Æthelwold!

[*Enter* ÆLFRIDA *on the left, followed by* ASE. *ÆL-*
*FRIDA* stands for a moment looking about her.]

ASE

Belike 'twas further on.

76

##### ÆLFRIDA

Nay, nay.  'Twas here.

[*Softly*]

Æthelwold!

[*She listens.*]

### ASE

It was a dream, I tell thee.
I had a dream myself.

##### ÆLFRIDA
[*Wildly*]

Ase, shall I choke thee,
Or wilt thou brank thy tongue?

[*Calling*]

Æthelwold!

[*She listens.*]

O God! how still it is, and empty here!
He is gone!   He is gone!
I shall never see him more!
Woe, woe is me!

[*She falls sobbing upon the ground.*]

##### ÆTHELWOLD
[*Off-stage*]

Out of my road!

MACCUS

*[Off-stage]*

And see thee run to thy death?   No, by the Body!
Madder than a wench with child thou art!
Nay, but I'll hinder thee!

ÆTHELWOLD

Out of my furrow, or I plow thee under!

*[He rushes in, followed by* MACCUS.]

Ælfrida!

*[He takes her in his arms.]*

ÆLFRIDA

My liefest heart!

ÆTHELWOLD

Now ring, ring, ring, ye hammers of wrath
On all the anvils of Doom!
Not less than all thy lightnings, O up-heavèd
      Heaven,
Can singe me now!

ÆLFRIDA

What wild words are these?

ÆTHELWOLD

Thou . . . thou . . .

78

Tell thy sweet beads twice over for our love,
And I'll be with thee.
Maccus, two words—
A black one and a white one.
[*He crosses to* MACCUS.]
Maccus, if I may trust thee as of old—

MACCUS

Fear not, my lord.
When thou wert wise, I did a wise man's bidding
Now thou art mad, I follow thy lost wits
A-gathering wool.

ÆTHELWOLD

Maccus, go back unto the King.
And say to him as follows:
[*He pauses, then continues rapidly*]
That I have seen the maiden,
And found her nothing fair.
A comely maid enough, and friendly-spoken,
But nothing for the King.

MACCUS

'Tis done, my lord.

ÆTHELWOLD

Further say:

79

[*He hesitates.*]

That whereas the Thane of Devon, the lady's
    father,
Is rich in lands and kine,
And whereas the Lord Æthelwold,
But for the King's love—

[*He stops short; then continues*]—

Sparing the King's love, hath little else beside,—
The blessing of King Eadgar is besought
Upon the wedding of Lord Æthelwold
Unto the maid Ælfrida.

### MACCUS

'Tis done, my lord.

[*He goes out on the right.*]

### ÆTHELWOLD

'Tis done.
'Tis done.

[*He goes up to* ÆLFRIDA *and, taking her into his arms,
    looks steadfastly into her face.*]

Now shall I look no more beyond thine eyes.

### CURTAIN

# THE KING'S HENCHMAN

## ACT III

[ORDGAR'S *house on the coast of Devonshire. The
following spring. A large room, though smaller than
the hall of* EADGAR *in Act I, and built throughout of
rough-hewn timber, the beams appearing enormously
thick and strong. The windows are hardly more than
loop-holes, the doors broad and low. In the left wall
is a door leading out into a courtyard which incloses
the kitchens, storerooms, and stables. Along this wall
run several open shelves holding bowls and jugs of
wooden and earthen ware. In the right wall, well toward the back, five broad steps of smooth stone lead up
to a landing and the door of* ÆLFRIDA'S *bower.
Further front along this wall is a large chest of carved
oak. In the back, the main door of the house, a huge
door taking up nearly half the wall space, stands open.
Through it can be seen dark ledges and the sea. It is*

*a bright, sunny morning.  On a settle at the left* ASE
*sits spinning with a distaff and spindle.* ÆTHEL-
WOLD *stands beside the door in the back wall, looking
out at the sea.*]

ASE

[*Singing*]

To cockles and thistles his acres are grown.
Dwindle, dwindle, dwindle, dwindle.
Mother-naked walketh alone.
Distaff, dwindle.   Fill up the spindle.
Nadder, nadder, making the bracken to wave,
Somewhere here, for I saw it once, is the
     Queen's grave.

ÆTHELWOLD

Ase, knowest thou where is thy lady?

ASE

Most likely with the steward, my lord,
What with the linen to buck,
And a new wench in.

ÆLFRIDA

[*Entering from the door at the left*]

Beshrew the house!

82

Full forty loaf-eaters,
And not a churl among 'em that knoweth his chore!

[*She goes over to the chest and kneels by it, lifting out
  some rolls of colored linen. Her hair is down
  her back in two braids. She is wearing an apron*].

## ASE

Thored is drunk again.
In he hove and would have me draw a thorn from
    his thick thumb.
But I would not.
And forth he went, buzzing like a fly in a crack.
Gone for good this time.

## ÆLFRIDA

Not likely.

## ÆTHELWOLD

[*Going over to* ÆLFRIDA *and standing beside her*]

Ælfrida, when shall I speak with thee?
We are never alone.
Always this woman, twisting, twisting the spindle
    at her thigh,
Or thy father,
Or some one else.

*83*

And I have that on my heart that I must share
    with thee.
Come with me down to the shore'

ÆLFRIDA

What—now?

ÆTHELWOLD

Now.  Now.

ÆLFRIDA

I know not how I can come now.
Morning's a busy time.
Canst thou not tell me tonight?

ÆTHELWOLD
[*After a pause*]

Sweet heart . . .
At night . . .
At night I can tell thee nothing.
Thou knowest how it is with me . . .
The sight of thy white shoulder through thy
    heavy hair
It maketh me to quake and sweat as in the first
    days.
What I was
Before I met thee

I forget.
What I am now
It needeth not a seer to see:
Thy hand,
Thy foot,
Love's churl.
Ælfrida, ere the last timber of my manhood be
    eaten through by love,
There's something I must tell thee!
Come with me down to the shore!

ÆLFRIDA
[*Rising*]

Softly, softly, my lord.
Thou must not shout so.
I will come.
Do thou go before, and bide by the spar in the
    shingle.
I've but to yield the keys to Ase, and I'll be with
    thee.

[*She goes over to* ASE. ÆTHELWOLD *goes to the door
    and looks out at the sea.*]

ÆLFRIDA
[*Giving* ASE *the keys*]

Ase, thou'lt find in the kitchen a fat wight,

*85*

Sucking her lip and cooling a pot of peas-broth,
Daft as a culver.
Run thither, ere she 'gin a-cooing to herself,
And set her to swilling the milk-pans.

### ASE
[*Rising*]

I'll handle her.
[*She goes out on the left. ÆLFRIDA returns to the
chest and kneels by it, replacing the things she
has taken out.*]

### ÆTHELWOLD

The tide is swelling back,
Bringing the winter wrack,
And shoving the red weed up the stones.
I never leave thee, but I feel 'tis for a long time.
[*He turns and looks at her.*]
Ælfrida!
[*She looks around at him, still kneeling.*]
Lovest thou me?

### ÆLFRIDA

Oh, ask me not of a morning if I love thee!—
When my mind is full of thimbles and churns!
I tell thee, so long as we bide here in my father's
house,

I am my father's housekeeper,
And thou shalt see me seldom but as a warder of
    cupboards and chests
And a doler-out of heal-alls!
Body of me!
[*She rises, leaving some of the linen still on the floor.*]
Am I to bide forever here,
Like a winkle stuck to a stone,
And die in the house I was born in?
Sick and sick to death I am
Of the stink of fish on the wharves,
And the squawk of seagulls,
And the wind that blows always!

### ÆTHELWOLD

Oh, God!—the wind that blows always!
Would I could put an arrow in the heart of the wind,
And bring his beating feathers down!
On that day,
On that day when the wind lay dead,
And the sea was smelt and smooth,
A man might think his thought out.

### ÆLFRIDA

Thy speech is a thread full of knots.
And thy deed likewise.

*87*

I see thee go forth into the wood to hunt,
And come home like a baby with a wilted blossom
    in thy fist.
Thy helmet is a house for spiders,
And thy saddle is cold.
Where is that Æthelwold
That was the King's darling,
And the dread of the Dane,
And my true love?

ÆTHELWOLD
[*In a pained voice*]

Ælfrida!
[*He turns away his face.*]

ÆLFRIDA
[*Coming up to him and putting her arms about his
    neck*]

My dear!   My dear!
Take me away from this God-forgotten spot!

ÆTHELWOLD
[*Quietly, removing her arms gently from about his
    neck*]

I will.
And that ere sundown.
   *88*

[*Enter from the left* ORDGAR. ORDGAR *is a short,
thick-set man of fifty, with the red face and neck
of a man who for years has eaten well and been
much out of doors. He is shrewd, but slow-
witted. His manner is by turns hearty and surly.*]

### ORDGAR

Good morrow, daughter and son!

### ÆLFRIDA

Good morrow, my father.

### ÆTHELWOLD

God give thee good day.
God give us all a good day.

### ORDGAR

'Tis weather like this will dry up the wooze
And give us the roads again.
They say that but for a stretch or two of puddle and
    addle,
And the swollen fords,
The way from here to Winchester's as clean as a new
    knife.
Ah, well, thou'lt soon be riding off to the King-Stool,
And my daughter with thee.

*89*

ÆLFRIDA

[*Proudly and excitedly*]

Yea, so!   And that ere sundown.

Shall we not, my lord?

Thou art the King's friend, and his foster-brother.

In Winchester we should be bidden to eat at the
    King's board;

And like as not have a house of stone with glass in
    the windows!

And I should be second to none but to the Queen
    that's dead.

ORDGAR

[*To* ÆLFRIDA]

"A house of stone," thou sayst.

And what art thou to be sneezing at the house where
    thy mother gave birth to thee?

Do thou keep out of this.

[*To* ÆTHELWOLD]

My son, when thou hast again the King's ear,

Forget not to put a flea in it for me.

ÆTHELWOLD

I know.   I know.   I'll not forget.

I must go out now and have a word with my men.

ORDGAR

*[Catching him by the sleeve]*

Say to the King:
"Thou hast in thy Thane Ordgar a good man and a
    knowing one
For Ealdorman of Wessex west of Wiltshire."

ÆTHELWOLD

I know.   I know.   I'll tell him.

*[He goes out left. ÆLFRIDA goes to the chest and
    kneels there, putting back what linen remains
    on the floor.]*

ORDGAR

*[To ÆLFRIDA]*

Art thou a wedded wife in sooth,
Or art thou still a maid?

ÆLFRIDA

*[Calmly, without looking up]*

Thou knowest well I was wedded in Holy Church
Two sennights after Christ-His-Mass
*[Crossing herself]*
To Æthelwold, Earl of East Anglia.

ORDGAR

Then wherefore all this pranking of crimpèd hair

Adown thy back,
As thou wert still a silly girl?

ÆLFRIDA

[*Closing the cover of the chest and rising*]

Still harping on that string!
One 'u'd think my hair were a rope to hang the King,
The fuss thou makest o't!

ORDGAR

That may all be.
But I wonder what folk say of thee,
Seeing thee with thy hair down.

ÆLFRIDA

They say, "What lovely hair!"

ORDGAR

Yea, gibe at thy father.   It becomes thee well.
But I tell thee, a man that cometh to a cross-roads
Must turn his back upon the one way
To follow the other.
Thou, thou wouldst yield no thing.
Thou art that shrew-mouse of the world—a wedded
        woman
That will not settle down.

ÆLFRIDA
[*Angrily*]

My hair is mine own, I tell thee!
And no man shall put the shears to it!
Though every wife in England and the Isles
Go callow as a sheep new-shorn!

ORDGAR
[*Going toward the door in the back*]

Thou art a greedy woman,
And God hath his eye on thee.
[*He goes out.*]

ÆLFRIDA
[*Furiously*]

Old mouthy man!
But I'll be shed of thee!
Let me but once set foot in Winchester,
I am East Anglia's Lady—and never more
The Thane of Devon's daughter!
[*Enter ÆTHELWOLD from the left.*]

ÆTHELWOLD

Ælfrida, canst thou be ready by low water
To take horse and be off?

ÆLFRIDA

To Winchester!

ÆTHELWOLD

No.   Not to Winchester.

ÆLFRIDA

Oh, Æthelwold!

ÆTHELWOLD

Nay, wife.   And tease me not.
I do beseech thee, be of one will with me,
Till we be well on the road.
Winchester, Winchester is a man's town,
Full of shouting.
There is nothing there for thee—for thee and me
Nothing there.
Later, belike—one day, not now. . . .
Next year—or the year after. . . .
But give me time.

[*He hesitates.*]

Wouldst thou be seen at the King-Stool in thy
     last-year's weeds?
Hast thou no need to buy thee somewhat—a
     smock, or a stole,
Some freak or other—some new-fangle thing—
Ere the ladies of the King's house look thee up and
     down?

94

ÆLFRIDA

[*Thoughtful*]

It is true the only hood I have that halfway be-
comes me
Is worn no longer by the ladies of the town. . . .
And my pilch of spotted fell—I could do with a
new one. . . .
But where shall I buy these things but in Win-
chester itself?
Gloucester hath nothing!

ÆTHELWOLD

Nay, nay.   'Twas some outlandish cheaping-stead
I had in mind.
Say . . . Ghent in Flanders.

ÆLFRIDA

[*With astonishment and delight*]

Ghent in Flanders!
Great town of my many dreams!
Why, lo, thou—thither to fare,
That would I rathest of all things under the welkin!

ÆTHELWOLD

Even so I.   Even so I.

*95*

I would liefer see the gray water widen 'twix us and
    England
Than aught I know.
[*Enter from the left* ASE.]

ÆLFRIDA

Ase! Ase!
Drop thy burthen to the floor,
And let the pots boil over,
And the wenches drown in suds,
And do thou fly and lade my boxes and chests
    with all that's mine!

ASE

Fare we forth?

ÆLFRIDA

We leave this house tonight for Ghent in Flanders!

ÆTHELWOLD

God willing.

ASE

For Ghent in Flanders!
And half thy linen i' the lye-buck!
[*She hurries out, left.*]

ÆLFRIDA

Oh, Devon, Devon!
Farewell, thou bitter strand!

*96*

## THE KING'S HENCHMAN

### ÆTHELWOLD

England, farewell, farewell,
Thou green and rainy land.
Never more, even with the mind's eye, must I
    behold
The empty heath, and the brown bracken under
    the sunset. . . .
The windy downs, where the hawthorn and the
    thorny gorse
Grow stinted and small. . . .

### ÆLFRIDA

Farewell to you, ye weeping fisherwomen,
Stopping your nets by the sea!
Ye shall behold me no more
With clutchèd kirtle climbing the slimy stones!
Yea, by the bones
Of Saint Ives and Saint Audrey,
Ye have seen the last of me!

### ÆTHELWOLD

Dear land, farewell to thee.

### ÆLFRIDA

Henceforth in sighing silk

97

And gossamer I go,
Hooded in beaver-fell, and shod in leather toolèd
   fair—
Such lordly weeds as the ladies of Flanders wear!

ÆTHELWOLD

Yea, there,
Unfretted there,
Shall I watch thee preen thy rainbow feathers,
Bright bird of my heart.

[*They go together to the open door, and stand looking
   out.*]

ÆLFRIDA

Chary days of grim and stingy winter,
Ye are broken, ye are strown!
Well come, thou singing high-day, thou blossomy
   sweet summer,
Thou lovely land unknown!
Open thy gates, thou mighty cheaping-stead!
Let every shop and stall with wondrous wares be
   hung!

ÆTHELWOLD

Oh, let us wander far! Oh, let us live forever!
The world is wide, and we are hale, and we are young!

[*They stand with their arms about each other, looking*

98

*out over the sea. The sound of rapid hoofbeats is
heard from the courtyard without.* MACCUS
*enters from the left, out of breath, and spattered
with mud.*]

### MACCUS

My lord!   My Lord Æthelwold!

[ÆTHELWOLD *and* ÆLFRIDA *turn.*]

### ÆTHELWOLD

What wouldst thou?

[*In alarm*]

Maccus!

[*Striding over to him and taking him by the arm*]

Thou'st evil tidings!

### MACCUS

The King is at our gates!

### ÆTHELWOLD
[*Crying out*]

'Tis come!

### MACCUS

Up the road he is, a mile or two beyond the swine-
herd's cot,
With a great threat of men, talking and laughing
and cooking breakfast.

*99*

At first I thought, "He hath got wind of it! Some
    blabbing ear-wig hath been at him!"
But nay, their talk was merry, and nothing evil in't.
Meseems he cometh not to bewray thee.
But only to bid thee good speed.

ÆTHELWOLD

God forgive me my sin!

MACCUS

God aside, what are we to do, my lord?

ÆLFRIDA

[*Who has caught the last words, coming forward*]

This ye are to do: ye are to make an end of all this
    humming and runing like two thieves in a
    hedge,
And tell me what is toward!

[ÆTHELWOLD *and* MACCUS *look at her without speak-
    ing.* MACCUS *bows his head and goes out, left.*]

ÆTHELWOLD

Oh, to be a fox in a trap!—
That I might gnaw my foot off and be free!

Lo, thou—down this road come riding through the
    sunny morning,

Three dark riders abreast:
The King, and Shame, and Doom.

### ÆLFRIDA

The King, thou sayst? Bound hither? To this
    house?—
And I in my barm-cloth!
[*She unties her apron.*]

### ÆTHELWOLD

Yea, make thyself more fair!
[*He takes her by the shoulders.*]
Ælfrida, swear, swear—
Ere ever the waters rise,
And stop the mouth, and hide the eyes,
And Love be a shriek in the ear that hears nothing,
    nothing!—
Swear thou wilt not forget the love that was be-
    tween us,
How sweet it was.

### ÆLFRIDA

Forget—our—love?
Art thou gone mad, to say it?

### ÆTHELWOLD

Hark—Hearest thou nothing?

*101*

ÆLFRIDA

'Tis but the wave in the hollow ledge.
The tide is high.

ÆTHELWOLD

High tide.  The sea is at a standstill.
The sea is at a loss which way to turn.
Woman! The mist that rises from the sea is not thy
    friend!
But for the mist, thou hadst been Queen of England!

[*Enter through the door in the back* ASE, *in time to hear
    these last words.  She retreats softly and remains
    standing just outside the door, listening.*]

ÆLFRIDA

Thou art mad!  Thou art mad!

ÆTHELWOLD

Hark what hath maddened me.

Hither I rode a little time ago . . .
A long time ago . . .
As henchman of the King,
On the King's business.
And this mine errand, lady—hearken well:
To seek, in the King's name,
And to woo, in the King's name,

And to betroth and pledge with the King's ring in
    the King's name,
Thee, thee, Ælfrida!—
Thee, but for the wretched love of a green and
    dizzy boy,
Queen of all Britain
And Lady of the Isles!

ÆLFRIDA

'Tis the long winter hath addled thy wits!
Me! Me! That have spent my days like a swallow,
Dipping in and out of a house in the eaves of the
    earth!
Me, Queen of Britain!

'Tis not true?

ÆTHELWOLD

[*Wearily*]

Yea, my child. 'Tis true enough.
Thou knowest in what way we met.
So . . . when I knew thy name,
I lied to Eadgar, saying thou wert all unworthy
    of so high a stead,
Being little fair,
And took thee for myself.

Oh, the good smack of truth on the tongue again,
After a winter of lies!

ÆLFRIDA
[*Coldly, after a short silence*]

Meseems, my lord, thou hast dealt wantonly by me,
And by my father,
And by the King.

ÆTHELWOLD

Thou under-sayst it.

ÆLFRIDA

Was there no time 'twix Candle Mass and Beltane
Thou mightst have told me this?

ÆTHELWOLD

Something always came in the way.

ÆLFRIDA
[*Musingly*]

But for thee,
I had been Lady of England
And bride of him that was rowed by the eight kings
      on the stream of Dee. . . .
But for thee,
I had waked of a morning to see

*104*

Great Eadgar, the Dove of Albion, and the Hawk
    of the Dane,
Asleep like a child in my bed. . . .
'Tis wonderful. . . .

ÆTHELWOLD

*[Passionately, turning on her]*

Sayst thou so?
Now, upon the Rood of Christ I swear,
He hath not got thee yet,
Nor shall he have thee whiles I live!
There never was a man so loved a woman
As I love thee.
Never in any world.
And that's to be reckoned with!
A year ago I had a good name among men.
Where is it now?
For love of thee, i' the swine-wash.
My plighted pledge—hang it for sale in the market,
Shall it fetch thee down a farthing?  Nay.
And such a friend as I had. . . .
Ywis, in the Month of the Wolves I wedded thee,
And thou shalt rend me yet;
But mine thou wert ere ever I knew thy name—
And that's to be reckoned with!

There, there thou shinest like a sun, filling the
    room!
Make haste, and hide thee in a cloud from the
    King's eyes!

[*He stares at her fiercely. Suddenly, as he looks at
her, his eyes narrow and he strikes his fist into
the palm of his hand.*]

Yea, by the Tree, one path is left us!
And thou shalt tread it for my sake, and for the
    love that thou sworest!
Go now, and darken thy cheek with the sap of the
    walnut!
And dust thy hair with the meal of the wheat!
Be foul!  Be bent!  Be weathered!
And keep thy bower,
That none may see thee
But myself and the King.

Is it much to ask of thee—to dim for a short time
    only thy shining?—
Yet many a wife hath done as much and more,
To shield from death her man,
And him no better than me!

ÆLFRIDA

From death?

*106*

ÆTHELWOLD

Why, yea.   What wouldst thou?
My life is not worth the life of a sheep-killing dog,
If thou go back on me.
But that is the least of my cares.   For if thou go
    back on me,
Thou lovest me not,
And Death were a small thing then.

[*The sound of a hunting-horn is heard in the near
    distance.*]

ÆLFRIDA

[*Bursting into tears*]

Oh, sorry me!   That must keep my bower like a
    naughty child,
The day the King comes!
Oh, sorry, sorry me!
That the King should see me looking loathsome,
With locks unkempt, and dusty with hateful meal!

Natheless
[*She wipes her eyes.*]
I will do it.
I go.

But thou—

Beshrew me, husband, thou lookest dreadful!
I' God's name, if thou wouldst blear the King's eye,
Tease a little blood to thy cheek
And see to the thongs of thy hose!
Thou lookest like a man washed ashore.

[*She turns to go up the steps to her bower.*]

[*Enter from the back* ORDGAR, *very happy and excited.*]

ORDGAR

Daughter!  Daughter!  And thou—
Moping here!
Heard ye not the horn?

ÆTHELWOLD

I heard it.

ÆLFRIDA

I heard it.

[*The marching-song of* EADGAR'S *men is heard faintly.*]

Men of EADGAR

Oh, Cæsar, great wert thou,
    And Julius was thy name,
That furrowed thy way through a fallow spray,
    And to stormy Britain came!
But I would not stand in thy stead,
For I'd liefer be quick than dead!

*108*

ORDGAR

Hark! 'Tis the King! 'Tis Eadgar!

Out! Out! And meet him on the road!

[*To* ÆLFRIDA]

Thou, thou half-wit!

Wouldst have the King see thee looking like a bundle untied?

Go! Do on thy holy day weeds! And be quick about it!

ÆLFRIDA

Not I. I am sick. I swoon.

Ase! Ase!

I go to my bower. And I come not forth.

[*Enter* ASE, *and supports* ÆLFRIDA *up the steps toward the door in the right wall.*]

ORDGAR

I might have known it! Was ever so willful a hussy as thou!

Couldst thou not be sick of a fast-day?

Well—so much for thee, then.

[*To* ÆTHELWOLD, *wheedlingly, taking him by the arm and urging him toward the door in the back.*]

Thou, my son—knowest thou thou art my dear son?

Yea, I dote on thee. I do, i' sooth.

ÆTHELWOLD

[*Turning his head*]

Ælfrida!

ORDGAR

Nay, let her sulk it out!
Mind thee—a little flea in's ear . . .
For Wessex west of Wiltshire!

ÆTHELWOLD

I know.  I know.  Ælfrida!

ORDGAR

[*Drawing him through the door*]

Thou knowest!  Ho, ho!  Thou knowest!
Trust thee!  What a day!  What a day!
'Tis a great day for Devon!

[*They go out.*]

[ÆLFRIDA *and* ASE *are standing on the landing leading
to* ÆLFRIDA'S *bower.*]

ASE

[*Fiercely*]

Thou'lt do no such thing!

ÆLFRIDA

Oh, Ase, thou knowest not wherefore—

ASE

Yea, but I do, then. For I stood with mine ear to
the door.
And such a shameful tale as I heard!
Hast thou no bone i' thy back?
Starch thy mind.
Thou must drop thy silver shell, to pick up the gold
one.

[*They go out.*]

MEN OF EADGAR [*nearer*]

Oh, Cæsar, great wert thou,
  And Hadrian was thy name!
Thine eye did itch till a Roman ditch
  Was dug in British shame!
But I would not stand in thy stead,
For I'd liefer be quick than dead!

[*During the song a crowd of villagers, fishermen, etc.,
run past the door in the back, calling and laughing. Their conversation and the song go on at
the same time.*]

A SADDLER

Lor', but I'm blown! I've run a mile, if an inch!

A FISHERMAN

Getting old, saddler!

*III*

A Neat-herd's Wife

All of a lather I am!

A Fisherman's Wife

Neighbour, what's that in thy hand, a gift for the
King?

A Miller's Wife

Bless my soul if it be not my goodman's shirt I was
a-wringing!

[*Laughter.*]

[*Several servants of* Ordgar's *household, among them*
Thored, *a pompous, drunken fellow, enter from
the left and run across the stage and out at the
back to join the others.*]

A Woman Servant

Thored! Thored! Think'st thou 'twill be the King
himself?

Thored

Ywis, 'tis the King himself!

[*They join the villagers running by.*]

A Blacksmith
[*In answer to* Thored]

Yea, and why not? What's amiss wi' Devon?

### A MILLER

That's the talk!

### SEVERAL VILLAGERS

Yea, what's amiss wi' Devon?

### SECOND FISHERMAN
[*To* BLACKSMITH]

Good on thy head, Wulf!

[*The hunting-horn is heard again, as if just outside the gate. A great shout goes up from the villagers off-stage.*]

### VILLAGERS
[*Off-stage*]

Eadgar!  Eadgar!  King of Britain and All the
  Lands About!
Be thou hale!  Be thou hale!  Be thou hale!

[*Reënter* THORED, *followed by servants and villagers.*]

### THORED

This way!  This way!  If ye'd see the hairs in's
  beard!
Hither he comes, I tell you!

[*The villagers climb upon the settles and chests and into
  all accessible high places.*]

*113*

THORED

[*To a man who is standing on a settle*]

Hoy, thou!  Hop down from there!  Leave un a
bench, man!

BLACKSMITH'S WIFE

[*To* BLACKSMITH]

Husband, husband, hoist the child to thy shoulder!

[*Looking up at the child*]

Ho, Wulfing!  Where art thou now?

SECOND WOMAN SERVANT

[*To* THORED'S *wife*]

Enid, thy cap's awry!

A YOUNG GIRL

[*Leading a very old man*]

Nay, father, none shall hide him from thee.

[*To villagers in front of her*]

If you list, let him through.

THORED

Here thou art, old un!  How are thine eyes?

OLD MAN

I shall see him.  I shall see him.
God be thanked, that hath spared me to this day.

*114*

THORED

Here he comes!   Now, then!   Ready!
All together wi' the "Eight Kings o' Dee"!

VILLAGERS
[*Grouped on the left of the stage and facing the door
in the back, singing*]

Malcolm of Cumberland, where art thou?—
Swinking at the oar, swinking at the oar!
Malcolm of Cumberland, where art thou?—
A-rowing of King Eadgar on the Stream o' Dee!

Kenneth of Scotland, where art thou?—
Swinking at the oar, swinking at the oar!
Kenneth of Scotland, where art thou?—
A-rowing of King Eadgar on the Stream o' Dee!
[*During the second stanza, enter* ORDGAR, *with* GUN-
NER, CYNRIC, *and other lords of* EADGAR'S *train.*]

VILLAGERS
[*Singing*]

Maccus of the Isles, where art thou?—
Swinking at the oar, swinking at the oar!
Maccus of the Isles, where art thou?—
A-rowing of King Eadgar on the Stream o' Dee!
[*At the end of the third stanza, enter* EADGAR *with his*

*arm about* ÆTHELWOLD, *in conversation with him. They are followed by* MACCUS, *other lords of* EADGAR'S *retinue, persons of* ORDGAR'S *household, etc.*]

VILLAGERS

Eadgar! Eadgar! Eadgar!
King of the English folk and Lord of the Isles!

EADGAR

God shield all here.

VILLAGERS

Well come, well come to Devon!
Kinsman and King, be hale!

ORDGAR

My King, if thou wilt do me the worship to break
bread in my house—

EADGAR

Nay, nay, I bid thee. We broke our fast but now,
and heartily.
Did we not, friends?

CYNRIC

Yea, so. Full as a tick are we all.

# THE KING'S HENCHMAN

## EADGAR

*[To Æthelwold]*

In sooth, I did not think when last I saw thee
I should see thee next a wedded man!

*[He seats himself upon the bench, left, and draws
Æthelwold down beside him.]*

Hast heard: there's a deal of barking and running
    about
Beyond the Severn?
Oh yea.
But said I: I ride not into Wales, but I ride by way
    of the shore,
And greet my brother ere the month be out.


Knowest thou, we have not met sithen St. Michael's
    Day?
Time flieth, 'tis said; but when I am afar from thee,
    friend,
He flieth with a wounded feather.


Yea, thou sorry knave!—and thou—
Thou hast not given me one thought
In all these giddy months!

AETHELWOLD

Not a day goes by
But I think of thee.

EADGAR

It warmeth my heart to hear it.

AETHELWOLD
[*Feverishly*]

Full oft I think—I think of the time when we were
    lads!
My mother's house in Mercia—
Dost mind thee, Eadgar, how the sun came through
    the door?
Meseems it never rained in those days!

EADGAR

'Tis a long time sithen.
[*He is silent, lost in thought.*]
Yea, my Lord Daft-Head—yea, my Lord Soft-Heart,
    it was like thee
To wed a maid no other man would have. . . .
But [*hastily*] I deem the tale hath fattened in the
    telling!
Howe'er it be,
My mind is set to love her for thy sake,

*118*

Though she be less fair than some.
Good sooth, a lissome body and a flashing eye,
These be not all!
I ween she hath a warm heart and a true heart,
And loveth thee more than well.

ÆTHELWOLD
[*In a strained voice*]

I thank thee, Eadgar.
[*He rises to his feet suddenly.*]
To ride into Wales, with a spear in the hand again!
And a shout in the blood again!
And an empty mind. . . .
[*He sinks down upon the bench.*]

CYNRIC
[*To* ORDGAR]

Thou'st a stalwart house here.

ORDGAR

It hath need to be.

EADGAR
[*To* ÆTHELWOLD]

Lad, let me look at thee.
[*Slowly, shaking his head*]

*119*

Say what ye will, 'tis little a man knows of his
    friend.
Even his hound shareth not its dream with him.
And thou and I—we have been long asunder.

Yea, yea—'tis a long time sithen.

Æthelwold, how is it with thee, lad?
In sooth and earnest tell me.
For thou hast in thine eyes a shadow that squeezeth
    my heart.

[*A little fair-haired serving-maid comes timidly for-*
    *ward with a tray, and stands at some distance*
    *from* EADGAR.]

ENID
[*Pushing her*]

Go on.   He'll not bite thee.

EADGAR

What hast thou there, child?   Is it for me?   Come
    hither, then.

CYNRIC

[*To* GUNNER *and* WULFRED, *looking at* ÆTHEL-
    WOLD]

Thou sayst it, man.

The woman's a shrew-mouse, or here's my sword to
    whittle tinder with!

#### EADGAR
*[To the child]*

Be not afeard, thou little honey-head.
I am no bee-wolf.
*[The child approaches.]*

#### WULFRED
*[Looking at ÆTHELWOLD]*

A home sick man, if ever I looked on one!

#### ENID
*[To the child]*

Wynna, speak up!   Art thou tongue-tied?

#### CHILD
*[Very frightened]*

If thee list, O King, 'tis elder wine.
'Twill be proud if thou drink it.

#### EADGAR

Why, then, here it goes.
*[He drinks.]*

GUNNER

[*Looking at* ÆTHELWOLD]

She feeds him too much fish.

[CYNRIC *and* WULFRED *laugh outright* **in a sudden gay shout**]

EADGAR

[*Giving back the cup*]

Thou'rt a good maid.
And what is more,
Thou'rt a winsome maid.

[*He turns to* ÆTHELWOLD. *The child runs back to her mother.*]

EADGAR

Now then.   This wife of thine—where is she?
Trimming herself, I ween;
Doing on her arm-rings.

ÆTHELWOLD

Nay. . . .
My wife is ailing. . . .
She cannot leave her bower.
Wilt thou be kind,
And wend thee thither with me,
To bid her good day?

EADGAR

Ailing, thou sayst? Why, man, I'm sad to hear that!
Ywis, lad, let us thither, and give her the gift I
   brought.
'Tis a wee thing, but belike 'twill gladden her eye.

[*They rise.* EADGAR *puts his arm about* ÆTHEL-
   WOLD'S *shoulders. They take a few steps across
   the stage to the door of* ÆLFRIDA'S *bower. The
   door suddenly opens.* ÆLFRIDA *enters, and
   stands on the landing.* ASE, *from without,
   quietly closes the door.* ÆLFRIDA *is dressed in a
   robe of richly embroidered silk. Her arms and
   hands are heavy with bracelets and rings of
   enamel and gold; she wears earrings and a neck-
   lace. Her hair is released from its braids and
   flows softly over her shoulders; about her forehead
   is a narrow fillet of gold. She is very pale,
   but so amazingly beautiful that even the villagers, who are accustomed to the sight of her,
   gaze at her admiringly.* GUNNER *and* CYNRIC
   *stare at her, open-mouthed, then exchange glances
   and turn their eyes upon* EADGAR. EADGAR
   *slowly lets fall his arm from* ÆTHELWOLD'S
   *shoulder.*]

123

ÆTHELWOLD

[*Crying out*]

Ah, Ælfrida!

EADGAR

So. . . .

So. . . .

[*He looks from* ÆLFRIDA *to* ÆTHELWOLD *in silence.*]

Why, then [*slowly*], my life hath been but a heaping
of sticks

Under an empty pot.

Soft—let me get my bearings.

In this light, no tree is where it stood.

Yea, in this wood

I must seek behind me what I hear before me.

And hold my bow with my other hand.

[*He is silent a moment.*]

To whom shall I hearken now, where four roads
meet?

In the church, or in the moot of wise men

Shall any tongue speak sooth?

Whom shall I set at the head of my fighters in an
evil time?

What hand shall I take?

Yea, for if thy tongue be forkèd, Æthelwold,

*124*

Then from sea to sea my kingdom hisses!—
And not a head is reared, but to strike at my heel.
I have broken my back to make a home for the
    slay-worm;
And kept the foe from her nest, that she might hatch
    her speckled brood.

[*He is silent again*]

What of my hope, then, and my high dreaming?
'Twas not for this I wrought, swinking and sweating
    like a hind at mine unwieldy char.
Like a hind? why, lo, ye,—the plowman coming
    home from the field at evening to his hearth and
    his ale
Hath stood to stare with open mouth upon me,
Still, still, in the failing light,
Hewing and heaving,
Setting stone upon stone,
Building England!

Idle, idle, all.

Wretched land, upon what hollow rafters fair to
    the eye
May not thy roof rest!

    [*To* ÆTHELWOLD]

125

Thou . . . thou . . .
I cannot take it in.
My mind, that hath been fed so long on the sweet
    fare of utter trust in thee,
Smells at this meat,
And turns away.

### ÆTHELWOLD

*[In anguish]*

Eadgar, Eadgar, what we have left to say must be
    quickly said!—
For lo, with thy sorrow and mine in the same room
The world heels over!
That hath been which could never be.
Here we stand at last, we three.
But the wind is too strong.   We cannot hear each
    other shout.
Did Love call out
When the wave went over his head?
For Love was one of us.
And I do not see him.

Do ye get what I say, Eadgar?   Ælfrida?   No?

*[He looks from one to the other beseechingly.* **EADGAR**
*stands with folded arms and immovable counte-*

*nance;* ÆLFRIDA's *face is whiter than linen, but
she does not look at* ÆTHELWOLD.]

So.

Shake your heads and laugh.

Let it go.

[*He draws his short sword, a weapon not much larger
than a dagger. Several of* EADGAR's *men step
forward.*]

ÆTHELWOLD
[*In a loud voice*]

Stand back from me!

Let no man start from his stead!

[EADGAR *lifts his hand, motioning his men to do
nothing.* ÆTHELWOLD *goes to the foot of the
steps and looks up at* ÆLFRIDA. *She is fright-
ened for herself and crouches back against the
door.*]

ÆTHELWOLD
[*Gently*]

Nay, nay—

Fear not, my dear.

I would not harm thee.

[*He looks steadfastly into her face.*]

'Tis for myself.

[*He stabs himself and falls near the foot of the steps.*]

127

ÆLFRIDA
[*With her hands over her eyes*]

Oh no!   Oh no!

MACCUS
[*Who has caught ÆTHELWOLD as he fell*]

Boy,
Was it for this I kept thy weapon bright?

ÆLFRIDA
[*Creeping fearfully down the steps and looking down
at ÆTHELWOLD*]

God in heaven,
How he bleeds!

MACCUS
[*Bitterly*]

He bleeds.
This that thou seest, splashed out in the dust like a
    bucket of kitchen slop,
Is a man's most dear blood.
He bleeds.
Stand back, pretty lady.
Look to thy weeds.

[ÆLFRIDA *draws back her dress instinctively and
    shrinks against the steps.*]

128

So.

I would not have thee foul this blood.

[*He turns away from her and looks intently into*
*Æthelwold's face.*]

My lord, my lord—speak!

Art thou there within thee yet,

Or art thou fled?

### EADGAR
[*Who has not moved from where he stood*]

Nay, Maccus. Lay him down. Lay him down.

What man hath met the thrust of Æthelwold

And spoke again?

He will not answer thee.

Nor me.

Not ever.

### ÆLFRIDA
[*Sobbing*]

Oh, most wicked me!

[*Bending over him*]

Æthelwold!

### MACCUS
[*Fiercely, half-rising*]

Stand back!

*129*

Or by the Body I'll do thee an evil!
For I hate thee with a full heart!

[*She cowers away from him, and sinks down upon
the steps, weeping.*]

### EADGAR

[*Coming forward and looking down at ÆTHELWOLD*]
Liest thou there in sooth?

[ÆLFRIDA *bursts into bitter sobbing.*]

### EADGAR

Have done, Ælfrida.
Thou hast not tears enow in thy narrow heart
To weep him worthily.
Wherefore have done.

Nor all of us here,
Nor all of England weeping,
Should weep his worth,
That was so young and blithe and bold,
Whom the thorn of a rose hath slain.

Wherefore let us hoard our tears for a little sorrow,
And weep not Æthelwold at all.

[GUNNER, CYNRIC, WULFRED *and other lords come
slowly forward, and stand about the body of*

130

ÆTHELWOLD. *Looking down at him, they chant, together with* EADGAR, *the Lament for the Untimely Dead.*]

### EADGAR
The ax ringeth in the wood.

### LORDS
And thou liest here.

### EADGAR
The boat shoves off from shore. The child
    of the boatman dippeth her hand in
    the sunny water of the sea.

### LORDS
And thou liest here.

### EADGAR
The horse standeth in the smithy door
    with lifted hoof, and shivers against
    the flies.

### LORDS
And thou liest here.


### CHORUS OF ALL THE PEOPLE
Woe—lo—woe!
Was it the wind in the tree?

He that spoke but now is no longer in the room.
Forth-farèd is he.

EADGAR

So.   Bear him softly hence.
And bury him deep, with his warm sword beside
    him.
Doughty of heart was he.
This day hath he dared two kings:
Myself and Death.

[GUNNER, CYNRIC, WULFRED *and* BRAND *take up
    the body of* ÆTHELWOLD *and bear it slowly out
    through the door, followed by* INGILD *and the
    other lords.*]

CHORUS OF PEOPLE

Woe—lo—woe!
Hearest thou the wind in the tree?
He that spoke but now is no longer in the room.
Forth-farèd is he.

CURTAIN.